Essentials
of
Anger Management

Shyam Bhatawdekar
Dr Kalpana Bhatawdekar

Essentials of
Anger Management

Books by Shyam Bhatawdekar and Dr Kalpana Bhatawdekar

1. **HSoftware** (Human Software) (The *Only* Key to Higher Effectiveness)
2. Sensitive Stories of Corporate World (Management Case Studies)
3. Classic Management Games, Exercises, Energizers and Icebreakers
4. Classic Management Games, Exercises, Energizers and Icebreakers (Volume 2)
5. Stress? No Way!! (Handbook on Stress Management)
6. **HSoftware** (Shyam Bhatawdekar's Effectiveness Model)
7. Competencies and Competency Matrix
8. Soft Skills You Can't Do Without (Goal Setting, Time Management, Assertiveness and Anger Management)
9. Essentials of Work Study (Method Study and Work Measurement)
10. Essentials of Time Management (Taking Control of Your Life)
11. Essentials of 5S Housekeeping
12. Essentials of Quality Circles
13. Essentials of Goal Setting
14. Essentials of Anger Management
15. Essentials of Assertive Behavior
16. Essentials of Performance Management and Performance Appraisal
17. Health Essentials (Health Is Wealth)
18. The Romance of Intimacy (How to Enhance Intimacy in a Relationship?)
19. Good People: *Novel, a refreshingly different love story*
20. Funny (and Not So Funny) Short Stories
21. Stories Children Will Love (Volume 1: Bhanu-Shanu-Kaju-Biju and Dholu Ram Gadbad Singh)
22. Travelogue: Scandinavia, Russia

To Our Family

Shyam Bhatawdekar   Dr Kalpana Bhatawdekar

Anger is largely a negative emotion. Unbridled anger can do serious harm to the person who gets angry. It may also harm the person or the event you are angry with. Extreme as well as frequent anger can deteriorate your overall health pretty hopelessly and make you do quite nasty things that are not in line with your usual characteristics.

This makes a strong case for "Anger Management". Everyone must learn how to control and manage one's anger. Managing anger not only keeps you away from its dangers but also results in many benefits.

Therefore a thorough knowledge of "Anger Management" becomes imperative. To facilitate gaining the knowledge in this vital subject in the shortest time, authors Shyam Bhatawdekar and Dr Kalpana Bhatawdekar included only the "essentials" of "Anger Management" in the book.

The authors are top-notch business executives, successful entrepreneurs, highly sought after business and management consultants, eminent management gurus and scholars, authentic human behavior experts and prolific authors. And so the book becomes an authentic document on the subject.

To read more by the authors, refer their websites: http://shyam.bhatawdekar.com, *http://writings-of-shyam.blogspot.com* and http://management-universe.blogspot.com

Essentials of

Anger Management

Shyam Bhatawdekar
Dr Kalpana Bhatawdekar

Published by Publishing Division of

Prodcons Group

8, Pranjal Society, Shiv Tirth Nagar, Paud Road, Pune
411038 (India)

Email: prodcons@prodcons.com

For other web publications, refer: http://management-universe.blogspot.com and
http://shyam.bhatawdekar.com

Contents

Essentials of Anger Management

Anger: Meaning

Human beings undergo many emotions from time to time. A long list of human emotions is given at the link http://emotion-feeling.blogspot.com/. Anger is one of such emotions. And it's a very powerful emotion. If not handled appropriately it can result in destructive and harmful impact on self and others including the loved ones.

We can categorize all the human emotions in two broad categories: positive emotions and negative emotions. By and large anger is a negative emotion except in certain few circumstances where it can be used as a driving force or for self-defense.

Basically it is an emotion of:

- Annoyance
- Irritation
- Fury
- Rage
- Antagonism

- Resentment
- Exasperation
- Maddening

Degrees of Anger

Anger ranges from mere irritation or momentary annoyance to extreme rage. Almost all the human beings get angry within this continuum. Therefore, it's pretty normal for human beings to get or feel angry.

Types of Anger

Generally anger can be classified in following types:

1. Anger experienced by ill persons because of the irritability caused by sickness
2. Anger due to irritability and frustration caused by the family members, other relations and professional or social associates not coming up to one's expectations
3. Anger due to some serious conflict or series of nagging conflicts or disagreements with family members and other associates

4. Anger that gets accumulated over a period of time due to series of unpleasant and unacceptable events

5. Anger felt out of helplessness and frustration in the face of personal misfortune

6. Anger arising out of meeting some unfairness in dealings with others or feeling exploited

7. Anger you feel justified with or as your right (self-righteous indignation)

Control Anger Before It Controls You

It's almost a cliché to say that even negative emotions like anger are quite normal or natural to human beings. But that does not mean that getting angry is a good habit. When you get angry frequently or whenever your anger is of high intensity those are the indicators that you should start controlling your anger and manage it appropriately.

When you are not in a position to control or manage your anger appropriately, it starts controlling you. Then your behavior with self and others may become harmful and destructive. Anger harms both the parties- the one who becomes angry and the one with whom you get angry.

In extreme anger situations you may lose total control over your mind. Under the pangs of the passion you may inadvertently commit certain acts that can be very drastic like getting into a physical fisticuffs, slapping, killings, accidents (at home or on roads).

Another equally serious condition of anger is internalizing the anger deep inside your system over long periods of time and brooding over it endlessly. This kind of simmering anger can have very detrimental effect on your physical, mental and psychological health. This may not only get you into serious physical ailments like increase of cholesterol levels, hypertension, heart conditions, ulcers and diabetes but also turn you into a negative person.

Therefore, you must learn to control anger before it starts controlling you. Do not turn a slave to this damaging emotion that is capable of:

- Reducing or interfering your social skills
- Disrupting your interpersonal relationships with your spouse, children and other family members
- Disrupting your interpersonal relationships with professional associates and social contacts

- Making you commit mistakes by impeding your ability to process the information and take decision
- Creating problems in carrying out your work and responsibilities related to professional, personal, family and social life
- Resulting in slower career growth and lost business
- Adversely affecting your physical, mental and psychological health in various ways
- Making you unhappy most of the time and slowing down or blocking the ability to remain cheerful
- Making you highly stressed most of the times
- Muddling your overall life

Extreme Anger Is Dangerous

Anger when pushed to extremes is only one letter short of danger. Wrath or extreme anger (also known as rage, frenzy or fury) can turn out to be very dangerous making you commit a behavior that could never be imagined from you. Many acts or crimes of violence or passion have their origin in extreme anger. You can end up doing things that is not your normal behavior. You lose your capacity of rational or logical thinking and behavior. It can consist of:

- Breaking or damaging things around you
- Bypassing or forgetting the habits of safety
- Hurling abuses, curses and insults on others
- Physically hitting a person(s) or harming a person(s) in any other physical way
- Plotting conspiracies against the person(s) with whom you are very angry and implementing them
- Attempting to harm self to the extent of trying to commit suicide
- Inadvertently succumbing to an accident at home, on roads and at office under the uncontrollable pangs of anger
- Killing one or many persons or committing any other serious offense or violence.

These behavior patterns are extreme in nature and if they persist over a significant period or are frequent they may need greater and special attention from a well-trained therapist or psychiatrist.

At times even small or insignificant incidents are capable of simulating a person excessively to making him edgy beyond control. Then he may give a major stress reaction to these seemingly small incidents. The examples are: road rage (motorway madness), airport rage (delays at airport), desk/office rage (violence at workplace), rejection/abandonment rage, rage built up from daily disappointments (long lines, excessive waiting, inefficient bureaucracy, callous or indifferent behavior of service providers etc).

Objective of Anger Management

Therefore the objective or goal of managing the anger should be to ensure that your anger is contained or moderated or managed such that you do not get harmed or harm others in any of the ways depicted in the foregoing paragraphs.

By managing the anger in an appropriate way, you stop reacting uncontrollably towards the events, systems and people responsible for your anger. Then instead of *reacting* you learn to *respond* to them more effectively. You can learn to moderate your degree of excitement or emotional upheaval. You can even learn to act (show) angry rather than really get angry. You can thus stop or minimize the damages that the anger and the resultant unbridled reactions may trigger.

Manifestations and Effects of Anger

Anger, basically a negative emotion is associated with physiological and psychological changes.

Anger triggers fight or flight response in the body. Anger is often used as an immediate defense mechanism against any perceived threat. Level of energy hormones, adrenaline and noradrenaline go up. The heart rate, blood pressure and respiration rate also go up. The mind feels alert but loses sense of reasoning.

When you get angry, you lose much more than just your temper.

When a person gets angry, he gets affected in some or all of the following ways:

- Change in facial expressions- contorted face, clenched or bared teeth, staring countenance
- Change in body language
- Aggressive actions
- Loud or cold voice

- Internalizing the anger, boiling inside but not expressing
- Increased stress and anxiety
- Insomnia
- Headache
- Digestion problems
- Increase in heart rate
- Increased cholesterol level particularly the bad or LDL cholesterol
- Increase in blood pressure
- Increase in level of adrenaline and cortisol
- Heart attack
- Stroke
- Depression
- Impairs ability to process information
- Impairs ability to listen
- Impairs prudence and objectivity
- Reduces empathy towards others and may cause harm to them
- Increases sugar and cholesterol levels

In summary anger not only ruins your day but shrinks your life span.

Causes of Anger

The factors given below are the main causes of getting angry:

- Expectations from others (including organizations) are not met
- Expectations from self are not met
- Feeling of being exploited
- Sense of being victimized
- Abuse (physical and verbal) by others
- Been insulted or feeling of being insulted or humiliated
- Disagreements or conflicts with others
- Feeling frustrated over the events or systems on which you have no or very little control (an incompetent boss, inefficient bureaucracy, disruptions of all kinds of preset events and systems, prolonged illness of self or that of near and dear ones, loss of job due to circumstances beyond your control, financial burden etc)
- Recall of the past deals and circumstances that were unreasonable, unfavorable and traumatic to you

Ways of Dealing with Anger and Their Outcome

When a person gets angry he normally deals with the anger in one of the four modes either intentionally or involuntarily:

1. **Suppress:** Persons who suppress their anger do not vent it out or talk about it with anyone. The anger keeps working inside their system and often works against them. It then results in blood pressure, heart disease, ulcers and depression. Though a bit controversial, people tending to be outwardly pleasant and peaceful but finding it difficult to express the negative emotions like anger tend to internalize their anger and are more prone to cancer. This type of personality is termed as type C personality.

   At times some persons convert their suppressed anger positively by not brooding over it endlessly but directing or focusing their anger on some meaningful actions. This is far healthier than allowing the anger to simmer inside.

2. **Wrong actions and/or wrong word:** Some persons when angry immediately react by becoming aggressive. This reaction makes them commit some wrong action and/or makes them speak out in an unpalatable language. This kind of thoughtless action results in regret or pseudo-justification which in turn results in strained relations, ill feeling, guilt and loss of self-esteem. This kind of explosive anger expression may also lead to overall poor health and even untoward cardiovascular events.

3. **Ventilate or express harmlessly:** Persons who are a bit assertive verbalize their anger in venting it out on the person who has caused the anger. They do not act or communicate aggressively as in point 2 above. In a firm manner they tell the other person about their anger and what they really need. However they may not necessarily attempt to resolve the issue to their satisfaction. But they feel satisfied enough that they vented out their anger on the person who caused it. In some situations they may not vent it out on the person who caused the anger but may talk it out with someone else they feel like talking to or are comfortable with. The

anger gets dissipated harmlessly. This approach results in no tension/stress. However it may not solve the main problem that triggered anger.

4. **Calm, communicate and resolve:** Some people with more understanding of anger management try to understand the emotion or the anger feeling they are experiencing and decide to sort it out. They think over it and try to locate the issues that made them angry. They try to calm down externally as well as internally so that their anger subsides to some reasonable extent. Then they communicate with the concerned person or persons and try to resolve the issues. Rather than remaining angry with the person or the event that made them angry they concentrate on the issues involved. This approach results in resolution/solution, no tension/no stress and strengthening relationship.

Managing Anger

Prevention is always better than cure. If you can learn not to get angry- it provides an ideal situation. However that may not be always possible. But how to respond to the situations that elicit anger is under one's control. An appropriate and considered response is the well thought out and structured reaction and remains under self-control. Therefore you must learn how to control and manage your anger.

We give below various ways and means of managing the anger:

- Learn about various emotions a human being can undergo. Also refer: "Emotions" at http://emotion-feeling.blogspot.com/. Awareness of various emotions helps you to understand that human beings can undergo large numbers of positive and negative emotions. It also helps you to introspect the emotion you are currently experiencing at a given moment.

- Train yourself to start identifying your own emotions including your anger. This way you will be able to remind yourself that you are about to get angry or already getting angry and put a brake on it. Being proactive is any time better than being reactive.

- Try to use the rationale. Reason out with yourself that getting angry is basically harming you and not the person who is responsible for making you angry. Sticking to anger is like holding a heated stuff to throw it at someone else but hurting self in the first place. Also your bursting out with anger alone will not solve the problem or meet your objectives. So why get angry? At times the other person who was the cause of your anger might not have done things intentionally to annoy you or he may not even be aware that he did something to you to incite the anger.

- Try to get into a habit of removing the resentments or contempt towards others from your mind. Everybody and everything in the world is not picture perfect. People have their imperfections in one aspect or the other like they can be inefficient, clumsy, tardy, less knowledgeable, tired, ill etc. Everyone may not be highly efficient nor may possess the required flexibility and will to improve himself. Try to increase your tolerance level and learn to forget and forgive. Forgetting and forgiving may not be easy, yet one should learn to do it.

- Try to understand the normal causes of anger and how getting angry is harmful mainly to you and your relationships with others. And then recognize the trigger point(s) of anger and do not immediately react to any such stimulus of anger. (Also refer: "Emotional Intelligence" at http://emotional-quotient-intelligence.blogspot.com/).

- Try to understand the problem or event and also the person(s) involved. Instead of getting angry and expressing your anger say to yourself, "I don't wish to get angry because it will not only harm me in many ways but it may not even solve the problem." Then focus on how to solve the problem in coordination with the concerned person(s). Get into a dialogue with him without the undertones of your anger getting surfaced. Anger normally dampens or stops your listening capability. Keeping this in mind make deliberate attempts to listen what the other person has to say. Fight with the problem and not with the person.

- Also remind yourself that it is not always that every problem of yours will always get solved as per your requirements. You may have to face and live with the problem at least for some time to come or at times even permanently. Say to yourself, "Oh, it's just one problem. But many other things in my life are in my favor. So let me not blow it up beyond proportions and unnecessarily get upset with it." Such an attitude reduces the intensity of your frustrations and the resulting anger. You are changing the way in which the external things that are beyond your control affect you.

•   Start communicating with the person involved with the potential anger episode on an adult-to-adult basis. Stay on the issue and not pin down the person. Be assertive (but not aggressive) http://assertiveness-skill.blogspot.in/. Put forth your part of communication logically and not emotionally. Present the relevant facts and figures and desist from talking in general terms.

•   When you do get angry, remind yourself that you are getting angry. And you must do something about it constructively. Say to yourself, "I am getting angry. It's no good. I must take control over this anger episode."

- Say to yourself, "Stop, stop...." (It's your emotional stop button and press it when needed). This is the first step you can start with.

- Then say to yourself repetitively, "Cool down, take it easy, relax....".

- Many people advocate that counting backwards distracts you from the anger episode and helps you calm down. So start counting backwards from 100.

- Take deep breaths. In such situations stomach breathing is more effective than chest breathing. For more details on this refer: http://managing-stress-strain.blogspot.in/2012/01/stress-management-deep-breathing.html.

- Do not react immediately. Reactions are normally irrational and emotion filled and do not help solving the issues involved. Responding appropriately to any situation considering its various angles is a better approach but responding needs some more time.

- Always keep the harmful weapons like guns, pistols, knives etc under lock and key or place them where these are not accessible easily or promptly. Reaction to anger can motivate you to abuse these weapons harming other people. By keeping them in a not an easily retrievable location gives the necessary time to cool down.

- Move away physically from the place of anger episode. There is no point in delving with the issue or the other person when you are infuriated. Correct timing is important. In such a condition logic does not work and the things may get aggravated if tackled immediately.

- It may be good idea to engage yourself in some brisk physical activity or exercise that may automatically provide an outlet to your anger. Go to gym or take a brisk walk or run. Physical activities stimulate certain brain chemicals that can make you feel better and relaxed. Listening to some good music, watching a humorous movie or working in your garden may also have considerably moderating effect on your anger.

- Buy some time for arriving at the right kind of response. Sleep over the matter for some time and in certain cases even for few days. Just forget about the issues and the related persons or organizations during this transitory sleep over period.

- Later ponder over the matter in your own time and space. Consider all the angles, including others' points of view. Get all the relevant facts and figures.

- Try to understand the cause(s) of anger. It will be good idea to keep a diary of your anger episodes. Try to analyze your anger outbursts. Find out why and how you get mad at others.

- Try to solve/resolve those causes by yourself and taking others into account or seeking their involvement. Remember about using the adult-to-adult and logical communication method based on facts and figures as mentioned earlier.

- Learn the techniques of conflict resolution (Refer for details http://manage-conflict.blogspot.in/). Often times it's the conflict with others that gives rise to anger. Use the most appropriate conflict resolution technique that can prove be useful in a given situation. Assertiveness training can help you a great deal (For details on assertiveness, you may like to refer http://assertiveness-skill.blogspot.in/).

- Humor is a great antidote for anger. Many times looking at a potentially disagreeable person or an explosive situation in a lighter vein can help diffuse the anger intensity or block it totally. Learn to laugh it out- particularly the trivial issues of life that can be dissipated lightly without getting provoked.

- In finding out the solutions you may think of various alternatives. If one particular solution is annoying to you, you may think of other less annoying alternatives or the ones that will make you happy rather than angry.

- Regular physical exercises, adequate sleep (7 to 8 hours) at nights and proper nourishment are required to keep you physically and mentally healthy. Healthy person is likely to embrace and develop positivity, optimism and calmness in life. This way you learn to look at others with more understanding and do not feel irksome at the minor instigations. This does not make you feel threatened to use your anger as the immediate defense mechanism.

- Having a good social network facilitates sharing your concerns and irritants with your fellow members and if needed to vent them out harmlessly. This also provides the necessary support system. The intensity of frustration and irritations becomes tolerable.

- If you find that you are not in a position to use the above-mentioned steps all by yourself and you need some further training or counseling on it, do not hesitate to attend an authentic training program on anger management or seek counseling from a competent therapist or counselor. Professional help allows you to be guided by an expert who knows the issues better than you.

Acting Angry

Once you get mastery in anger management, you can use anger in a controlled manner. You can deliberately decide to get angry or not to get angry. The emotion "anger" is now your slave. It does not control you any more.

What it means is that now you can show angry or act angry without helplessly succumbing to getting angry without being aware of it.

At times you need to be firm to achieve the desired results from self or from others. Acting angry or showing angry in a controlled manner is a way of displaying your firmness. It may have salutary effects on achieving your objectives. Showing angry or acting angry uses your assertive behavior. You use your demeanor and firmness of voice appropriately to make a positive impact on the other person(s).

To do so you have to become greatly competent in anger management and assertiveness. We produce here Aristotle's quote in this connection, "Anybody can become angry- that is easy, but to be angry with the right person and to the right degree and at the right time and for the right purpose and in the right way- that is not within everybody's power and is not easy."

Benefits of Anger Management

Implementing what you learnt under "anger management" not only keeps you away from its dangers but also results in many benefits. Some of these benefits are given below:

- Rather than reacting to the person you start responding to the underlying problem about which you got angry. This allows good degree of introspection and that is very helpful in many ways.
- You get into a problem solving mode rather than remaining in the blaming game.
- By getting into proper dialogues and negotiations with the parties involved and solving the problem you may improve your interpersonal relationships.
- Controlled anger motivates you to confront the problematic situations with greater determination to solve them and meet your objectives.
- You physiological and psychological health may now improve rather than deteriorate.

- Your frustration level and the feeling of being exploited reduce a lot.

Teach Children

It is necessary that the parents teach their children how to manage their anger. When they learn the anger management in their childhood they will face less difficulties in their adult life.

Expressing anger appropriately is a learned behavior. Given below are some suggestions on how to train your children to deal with anger:

- Be the role model. Lead by example.
- Promote open and honest communication in the family.
- Tell them that anger is natural but they should express it in a proper way. Explain them what is a proper way.
- Explain the difference between aggression and anger.
- Then permit them to express their anger in appropriate way.

- Punish aggression or violence but not the appropriately expressed anger.
- Teach your child ways of remaining calm even under provoking situations. Also help them to learn how to calm down when they get agitated.
- Your child is a little person; listen to his side with patience and respect.
- Help your children to learn practical ways of solving problems.

Process of Problem Solving

You would have noticed that the anger management steps suggested in this book emphasize "problem solving" as one superior method to tackle your anger on a more permanent basis. It will be a good idea to brush up the following steps of practical problem solving process:

1. Recognize that a problem exists that is irksome to you. Take ownership of the problem.
2. Define the problem in consultation with the concerned persons.
3. Analyze the problem. By way of brainstorming along with the concerned persons and by collecting

the relevant facts and figures conceptualize the situation and find out the reasons of the problem.

4. Prioritize the causes. Some causes may be more important than the others and need to be tackled first.

5. Generate solutions so that all the important reasons for the problem are tackled first. Also try to cover the rest of the causes in the second stage. Take the concerned persons into account while developing the solutions.

6. Evaluate the various alternative solutions and pick up the best for implementation.

7. Implement the chosen solutions.

8. Review the solutions to make sure that they are actually solving the problem. Make corrections if required.

9. Review the outcomes.

10. Monitor the entire plan till the problem gets solved on a permanent basis.

www.ingramcontent.com/pod-product-compliance
Lightning Source LLC
Chambersburg PA
CBHW051418170526
45165CB00004BA/1867